crab recipes

ISBN: 978-1-257- 89896-1

For my family --

Ed, my husband who never gets tired of my cooking

Shampoo, my very talented artist

Ma-e, who shares my passion for cooking

Ibet, my legal adviser

Chaka, my dog

-- who made writing this cookbook

possible, meaningful,

inspiring, and enjoyable

TABLE OF CONTENTS

CHILI CRABS

4 crabs, top shell removed, cut into 4

2 tablespoons cooking oil

1 head of garlic, minced

3-5 chili peppers (siling labuyo), minced

1 red bell pepper, sliced

Spring onions, cut into 1" length

Salt and pepper

1. Heat oil in a pan and sauté garlic, chili pepper, crabs and red bell pepper.

2. Season with salt and pepper.

3. Stir-fry until done. Garnish with spring onion.

4. Serves 3-4.

Tip: Perfect as "pulutan" (beer session dish) with ice-cold beer. Other suggested side dish: chilled turnips sticks (singkamas).

CRAB ADOBO

4 crabs

½ cup vinegar

1/3 cup soy sauce

1 bay leaf

½ teaspoon black peppercorns

1 head of garlic, crushed

4 eggplants, roasted and peeled

1. Heat oil in a pan and sauté onion.

2. Add crab and stir-fry for 2 minutes.

3. Add vinegar, soy sauce, garlic, bay leaf, and peppercorns.

4. Cook in low fire until done.

5. Serve on top of roasted eggplant.

6. Serves 3-4.

Tip: Perfect dish to bring to the beach -- it won't spoil on a hot day. Suggested side dish: slices of green mangoes.

CRAB AND BAMBOO SHOOTS IN COCONUT CREAM

(GINATAANG LAMBAY AT LABONG)

2 coconuts, grated

2 tablespoons cooking oil

2 tablespoons garlic, crushed

3 tablespoons onion, chopped

2 tablespoons ginger, cut into strips

3 crabs, cut into halves

2 cups fresh bamboo shoots (labong), pre-boiled and drained

2 tablespoons vinegar

Salt

1. Extract 1 cup coconut cream and 1 cup coconut milk from the grated coconut. Set aside.

2. Heat oil in a pan and sauté garlic, onion, ginger and crabs. Cover and simmer for 2 minutes.

3. Add coconut milk and simmer. Add labong, vinegar and coconut cream. Do not stir.

4. Season with salt.

5. Simmer until sauce thickens. Serve hot.

6. Serves 3-4.

Tip: Fresh bamboo shoots are usually bought sliced. Be sure to remove the hard fibrous tissues. Wash very well and boil for 10 to 20 minutes uncovered. Drain and rinse in cold water. Canned bamboo shoots should be rinsed in hot water.

CRAB AND CORN SOUP

1 tablespoon cooking oil

3 tablespoons butter or margarine

1 tablespoon garlic, minced

1 cup crabmeat

2 cups corn, scraped from the cob

4 tablespoons cornstarch, dissolved in 2 tablespoons water

6 cups crab stock

Fish sauce (patis)

Pepper

2 eggs, beaten

1 tablespoon spring onion, chopped

1. Heat oil and butter in a saucepan. Sauté garlic, onion and crabmeat.

2. Add crab stock and let it boil.

3. Season with patis and pepper.

4. Add beaten eggs and stir with a fork to form threads.

5. Thicken with cornstarch dissolved in water.

6. Garnish with spring onion. Serve hot.

7. Serves 4-6.

Tip: Boil ½ kilo of crabs in 6 cups of water and fish sauce. Lower heat and simmer for 15 to 20 minutes. Remove crabmeat from shell and set aside. Reserve soup stock.

CRAB FRIED RICE

2 tablespoons cooking oil

2 tablespoons garlic, chopped

1 onion, chopped

1 cup crabmeat, flaked

½ cup peas

½ cup carrots, cut into small cubes

6 cups cooked rice

Salt and pepper

2-egg omelette, cut into strips

1. Heat oil in a wok and sauté garlic, onion, crabmeat and rice.

2. Add carrots and peas. Toss until well blended.

3. Season with salt and pepper. Serve hot.

4. Top with omelette strips.

5. Serves 4-6.

Tip: For a richer flavor of fried rice, use butter or margarine instead of cooking oil. You can also reserve half of the sautéed crabmeat to use as a topping for better plating.

CRAB GINATAAN WITH SITAW AND KALABASA

(CRAB IN COCONUT CREAM WITH STRING BEANS AND SQUASH)

2 tablespoons cooking oil

2 tablespoons garlic, crushed

2 tablespoons ginger, cut into strips

2 tablespoons onion, sliced

4 crabs, cut into halves

2 coconuts, grated

2 cups squash (kalabasa), cubed

1 bundle string beans, (sitaw) cut into 2" lengths

3-5 pieces hot chili peppers (siling labuyo), chopped

Salt

1. Extract 1 cup coconut cream and 1 cup coconut milk from the grated coconut. Set aside.

2. Heat oil in a pan and sauté garlic, ginger, onion and crabs.

3. Add coconut milk and simmer for 5 minutes.

4. Add string beans, squash and chili peppers.

5. Season with salt.

6. Add coconut cream. Simmer until broth is thick and oily. Serve hot.

7. Serves 3-4.

Tip: This is a perfect potluck dish -- very appetizing and colorful when served in glass servers.

MA-E'S CRAB KALABASA SOUP

500 grams crabmeat flakes

500 grams cubed squash (kalabasa)

4 tablespoons calamansi (Philippine lime) juice

2 pieces onion, roughly chopped

2 tablespoons lemongrass, chopped finely

300 ml. coconut milk

300 ml. all-purpose cream

300 ml. water

8 pieces kamias (bilimbi fruit), sliced

White pepper

Patis

Garnish:

   Dahon ng sili (leaves of the chilli pepper plant)

   Toasted garlic bread

   Kalabasa flowers (squash flowers)

1. Boil water, squash, lemongrass and onion in a pot until tender.

2. Blend in a processor or hand mixer until smooth.

3. Add calamansi juice, crabmeat, kamias, and coconut milk. Simmer gently over low fire.

4. Add cream. Season to taste.

5. Add kalabasa flowers. Garnish with sili leaves.

6. Serve hot and top with croutons.

7. Serves 4-6.

Tip: If you don't have crab, shrimps are a wonderful alternative. Make the shrimp broth in advance by boiling the shrimp heads (you can use its body for a different dish). Extract more flavor by crushing the shrimp heads. Just remember to run it through a strainer to remove all shells.

CRAB KARE-KARE

4 crabs boiled in 6 cups water

1 cup annatto (achuete) water

2 tablespoons garlic, crushed

2 tablespoons onion, chopped

6 cups crab stock

1 cup peanut butter or crushed roasted peanuts

1 cup toasted rice flour or grounded toasted rice

1 bundle string beans cut into 2" lengths

¼ kilo eggplant, sliced

1 banana heart, sliced

Bagoong alamang (shrimp paste)

1. Heat oil in a saucepan and sauté garlic and onion.

2. Add achuete water and crab stock. Bring to a boil.

3. Add peanuts and ground toasted rice.

4. Add crabs and simmer for 5 minutes.

5. Add eggplants, string beans and banana heart.

6. Simmer until all the vegetables are done.

7. Serve hot with sautéed bagoong alamang.

8. Serves 4-6.

Tip: Bagoong alamang can now be bought in tiny cans. The brand I use is by Barrio Fiesta.

CRAB MIKI SOUP

2 tablespoons cooking oil

1 head garlic, minced

1 onion, chopped

1 cup crabmeat, chunks

1 cup carrot, cut in small cubes

1 cup cabbage, sliced thinly

8 cups crab stock

½ kilo miki

2 tablespoons cornstarch dissolved in 1 cup water

3 eggs, beaten

Patis

Pepper

2   tablespoons spring onion, chopped

1. Heat oil in a saucepan. Sauté garlic until light brown. Remove garlic from oil and set aside.

2. Sauté onion and crab meat. Add crab stock and let boil.

3. Add miki, carrots and cabbage.

4. Season with patis and pepper. Thicken with cornstarch dissolved in water.

5. Stir in beaten eggs. Garnish with spring onion and fried garlic. Serve hot.

6. Serves 6-8.

Tip: Sometimes, adding a few slices of shitake mushroom adds more depth to the soup.

CRAB MOLO SOUP

2 cups crab meat

1 cup singkamas (turnip), finely chopped

2 tablespoons spring onion, chopped

1 teaspoon salt

1 teaspoon pepper

1 egg wanton wrappers

½ stick butter or margarine

2 tablespoons garlic, minced

1 cup onion, chopped

8 cups crab stock

2 hard-boiled eggs for garnish

Patis and pepper

1. In a bowl, combine crabmeat, singkamas, spring onion, salt, pepper, and egg. Mix well.

2. Stuff into wanton wrappers by spoonfuls. Set aside.

3. In a saucepan, heat butter and sauté garlic and onion.

4. Add crab stock and simmer. Season with patis and pepper.

5. Drop the wanton into the simmering stock. Cook until done.

6. Garnish with spring onion and slices of hard-boiled eggs.

Tip: If you have sesame oil, add a few drops to the crabmeat mixture.

CRAB OMELETTE

6 eggs, beaten and seasoned with salt and pepper

½ stick butter or margarine

2 onions, sliced

2 red bell peppers, sliced

½ cup mushrooms, sliced

1 ½ cup crabmeat, flaked

Salt and pepper

1. Heat butter in a non-stick pan. Stir-fry onions, mushrooms, bell peppers and crabmeat.

2. Pour in the beaten eggs. Cook until set.

Tip: For really creamy omelette, add a dollop of mayonnaise.

CRAB PANCIT BUKO

(CRAB AND YOUNG COCONUT NOODLES)

2 tablespoons cooking oil

2 tablespoons garlic, crushed

2 tablespoons onion, chopped

1 cup carrots, cut into strips

1 cup Baguio beans (green beans), cut diagonally

4 cups buko meat, cut into strips

1-cup crabmeat, chunks

1 cup buko (coconut) juice/crab broth

Patis and pepper

1.   Simmer crabs in buko juice until done. Remove meat and reserve broth.

2.   Heat oil in a pan. Sauté garlic, onion, carrots, Baguio beans, crabmeat. Set aside half cup for garnishing.

3.   Add buko meat. Pour in crab broth. Season with patis and pepper. Simmer until done.

Tip: To add a more festive feel to your dining table, surprise your guests by using the actual coconut shells as soup bowl.

CRAB POCHERO WITH EGGPLANT SAUCE

4 crabs, cut in half

2 tablespoons cooking oil

1 head garlic, minced

2 onions, chopped

2 cups tomatoes, chopped

2 tablespoons tomato paste

Salt and pepper to taste

2 pieces camote (sweet potato), quartered

8 saba (plantain bananas), peeled

1 small cabbage, cut in wedges

¼ kilo Baguio beans (green beans)

¼ kilo native pechay (Chinese cabbage)

Patis to taste

Eggplant sauce:

Combine in a bowl --

½ kilo eggplants, boiled, peeled and mashed

1 garlic, minced

½ cup vinegar

2 tablespoons sugar

Salt and pepper to taste

1. Heat oil in a saucepan and sauté garlic, onions, tomato, tomato paste and crabs. Add enough water to cover crabs. Simmer.

2. Add camote and bananas and simmer until half-cooked.

3. Add the rest of the vegetables and simmer.

4. Season with patis. Serve with eggplant sauce on the side.

Tip: Get more flavor from the eggplants by grilling it over charcoal instead of boiling them.

CRAB RELLENO

1 tablespoon cooking oil

1 tablespoon margarine

2 tablespoons garlic, minced

2 tablespoons onion, chopped

1 cup crabmeat, flaked

1 cup potatoes, diced

Salt and pepper

3 eggs

Breadcrumbs

Catsup

1. Heat oil and margarine in a pan and sauté garlic, onion, crabmeat and potatoes.

2. Season with salt and pepper.

3. Cook until potatoes are tender. Let cool.

4. Beat eggs and add to the crab mixture.

5. Pack into crabshells or form into patties.

6. Coat with breadcrumbs and fry until golden brown. Serve with catsup.

Tip: You can use the orange crab fat (aligue) for a second dish such as pasta aligue.

CRAB SANDWICH #2

1 cup crabmeat

1 cup white cheese

1 cup mayonnaise

1 tablespoon onion, chopped

1 tablespoon calamansi (Philippine lime) juice

½ teaspoon salt

½ teaspoon pepper

Mix and toss lightly. Spread on sliced bread or pan de sal. Garnish with thinly sliced apple.

Tip: This can also be used as a dip.

CRAB SANDWICH #3

1 cup crabmeat

1 cup butter

1 tablespoon garlic, minced

1 cup white cheese

Blend well and use as filling on sliced bread or as topping on crackers.

Tip: For variations, add minced parsley.

CRAB SANDWICH #1

1 cup crabmeat

1 cup white cheese

1 cup ripe avocado, mashed

1 tablespoon onion, finely chopped

1 tablespoon calamansi (Philippine lime) juice

½ teaspoon salt

½ teaspoon pepper

Mix all ingredients and toss lightly. Use as filling on sliced bread. Garnish with tomato and cucumber.

Tip: Instead of mashing the avocado, you can opt to slice it thinly then serve it as a garnish as well.

CRAB SINIGANG SA SAMPALOK

(CRAB IN TAMARIND SOUR BROTH)

2 tablespoons cooking oil

1 tablespoon garlic, crushed

1 tablespoon ginger, sliced

1 tablespoon onion, sliced

2 tablespoons ripe tomatoes, chopped

4 crabs, halved

1 radish, peeled and sliced

1 bundle mustard leaves

¼ kilo unripe tamarind, boiled in 4 cups water and mashed. Reserve the broth.

2 long chili peppers (siling haba or long green chilli peppers)

Patis

1. Heat oil in a saucepan and sauté garlic, ginger, onion, tomatoes and crabs.

2. Add radish chili peppers and mustard leaves.

3. Pour in the broth from the tamarind. Let boil and simmer until crabs and vegetables are done.

4. Season with patis. Serve hot.

Tip: Tamarind can be replaced with kamias (bilimbi fruit).

CRAB SIOMAI

1 cup crabmeat

2 cups singkamas (turnips) , finely chopped

½ cup spring onion, chopped

1 egg

4 tablespoons cornstarch

Salt and pepper to taste

Siomai (wanton) wrappers

1. Combine ingredients in a bowl and mix well.

2. Place 1 tablespoon of the mixture on each siomai wrapper.

3. Mold into shape.

4. Arrange in a steamer. Steam for 10 to 15 minutes.

5. Serve with soy sauce and calamansi dip.

Tip: For special occasions, you can put one quail egg in each siomai.

CRAB SQUASH OKOY

Batter:

½ cup flour

1 cup cornstarch

1 ½ teaspoon baking powder

1 ½ teaspoon salt

½ teaspoon pepper

¼ cup annatto (achuete) water

1 ½ cup crab broth

1 egg

Topping:

3 cups squash, cut into strips

½ cup onion, sliced

¼ cup crabmeat

Dip:

1 cup white vinegar

4 cloves garlic, crushed

½ onion, finely chopped

1/8 teaspoon pepper

¼ teaspoon salt

1 calamansi (Philippine lime)

1. Mix batter until smooth.

2. Add toppings.

3. Fry by tablespoonfuls in 1-inch deep oil until golden brown.

4. Serve hot with dip.

Tip: This is a popular street food in the Philippines. Usually, shrimps are used, not crabs.

CRAB SQUASH SOUP

1 tablespoon cooking oil

3 tablespoons butter or margarine

½ cup onion, chopped

1 cup crabmeat

4 cups squash, cubed

8 cups crab stock

Salt and pepper

1. In a saucepan, heat oil and butter, then sauté onion, crabmeat and squash.

2. Add crab stock and bring to a boil.

3. When squash is soft, mash with the back of a ladle or use blender.

4. Simmer until thick.

5. Season with salt and pepper.

6. Boil crabs in 8 cups water with 2 tablespoons fish sauce (patis) for 5 to 10 minutes.

7. Reserve stock for soup.

Tip: For an extra kick, add chili flakes.

CRAB STICKS

1 cup white cheese

1 cup turnips, chopped finely

1 cup crabmeat

Salt

Lumpia wrapper, small

1. Mix cheese, turnips, crabmeat and salt until well-
    blended.

2. Wrap by tablespoonfuls in lumpia wrapper.

3. Fry until golden brown.

Tip: If you have leftover lumpia wrappers, you can wrap cheese with
long green chili (seeds removed) to make "dynamite", a popular
street food in Pampanga City.

CRAB TINOLA WITH MALUNGGAY

(*CRAB WITH MORINGA LEAVES*)

2 tablespoons cooking oil

2 tablespoons garlic, crushed

2 tablespoons ginger, cut into strips

3 crabs, cut in halves

2 cups unripe papaya, peeled and sliced diagonally

3 cups water

1 cup malunggay (moringa) leaves

Patis

1. Heat oil in a saucepan and sauté garlic, ginger, onion and crabs.

2. Simmer for 2 minutes.

3. Add papaya. Cover and simmer for another 2 minutes.

4. Add water and simmer until papaya is done.

5. Season with patis.

6. Add malunggay leaves. Serve hot.

Tip: Malunggay is an inexpensive source of vitamins A, B, C and calcium.

CRAB WITH UBOD NG NIYOG

(FRESH LUMPIANG HUBAD)

1 kilo ubod ng niyog (heart of the coconut tree), cut into strips

2 tablespoons cooking oil

2 tablespoons garlic, minced

2 tablespoons onion, chopped

1 cup crabmeat

1 cup crab broth

Patis

Pepper

1 cup roasted peanuts, roughly chopped, mixed with

2 tablespoons sugar

SAUCE:

½ cup brown sugar

1 tablespoon soy sauce

2 cups crab broth

1 teaspoon salt

2 tablespoons cornstarch

2 tablespoons garlic, minced

1.   Mix and boil until thick. Add garlic after cooling a few minutes.

2.   Heat oil and sauté garlic, onion and crabmeat.

3.   Add coconut ubod and season with patis. Add crab broth and cook in low fire until almost dry.

4.   Serve hot, topped with peanuts and sauce.

Tip: Usually, this dish is wrapped in egg roll or lumpia wrapper. For this recipe, we didn't wrap it so it's called "lumpiang hubad". In Filipino, "hubad" means naked.

MA-E'S CRABS IN GINGER TURMERIC SAUCE

4 crabs, cut in half

1 stick butter or margarine

1 head of garlic, peeled and chopped

Leeks or spring onions, sliced

4 tablespoons luyang dilaw, roughly chopped

Sugar, patis (fish sauce), oyster sauce, ground pepper to taste

1 teaspoon ground turmeric

1-2 cups crab stock

Cornstarch to thicken sauce

1 sili labuyo (chilli pepper) chopped

Optional: tenga ng daga (black ear fungus) / shitake mushrooms

Garnish: coriander / wansoy

1. Melt butter, then sauté turmeric ginger and garlic until fragrant.

2. Add mushrooms and crabs. Set aside.

3. Add stock, patis, sugar and oyster sauce. Season to taste.

4. Add leeks and sili.

5. Add cornstarch dissolved in water to thicken.

6. Pour sauce on cooked crabs.

7. Garnish with wansoy.

Tip: If you have it, use fresh turmeric (yellow ginger). It'll give your sauce a nice yellow-orange color, too.

CRABS WITH YOUNG COCONUT

(*LAMBAY SA BUTONG*)

3 crabs, cut in half

3 camote (sweet potato), quartered

½ cup sliced tomatoes

½ cup sliced onions

1 cup sliced kamias (bilimbi fruit)

1 teaspoon black peppercorns

2 young coconuts (scrape meat, reserve juice)

Patis to taste

1. In a saucepan, combine all ingredients and bring to a boil.

2. Lower heat and simmer for 15 minutes.

3. Season with patis.

MA-E'S CREAMY CRAB SALAD

750 grams crabmeat

1 pack real mayonnaise

1 pack all-purpose cream

1 cup yoghurt

350 grams potatoes, quartered

200 grams celery, chopped into cubes

200 grams carrots, small cubes

250 grams beets, small cubes

1 bar of cheese, small cubes

6 cloves garlic, grated

1 onion, minced

Salt and pepper

Garnish: mixed greens

1. Pre-cook potatoes, carrots, beets. Dont overcook.

2. Combine crabmeat, celery, carrots, potatoes, beets and cheese.

3. Prepare dressing in a separate bowl. Blend the mayo, all-purpose cream, yoghurt, and garlic well. Take care not to add too much garlic. Season with salt and pepper.

4. Combine dressing with the crab mixture.

5. Toss lightly. Chill before serving.

Tip: If you like your dressing to have a savory and sweet flavor, use roasted garlic. Cut-off the top part of your garlic head, drizzle oil and add salt and pepper, then wrap it in foil. Roast until you can easily squeeze the creamy garlic from the cloves. This is also great for pasta sauces.

CREAMY CRAB SOUP

1 tablespoon cooking oil

3 tablespoons butter or margarine

½ cup flour

2 cups fresh milk

6 cups crab stock

Fish sauce (patis)

Pepper

1. In a saucepan, heat oil and butter.

2. Add flour and stir till smooth.

3. Pour in crab stock. Boil.

4. Slowly pour in milk while stirring.

5. Simmer until soup thickens.

6. Season with patis and pepper. Serve hot.

Tip: Add various vegetables for texture and flavor.

MA-E'S CRAB FRIED RICE SPECIAL

1 stick butter or margarine

½ cup chopped onion

¼ cup chopped tanglad (lemongrass)

½ cup minced garlic

2 teaspoons white sugar

2 teaspoons banana catsup

4 tablespoons tomato sauce

¼ cup oyster sauce

1 kilo day-old cooked rice

750 grams crabmeat, chunks

3 eggs, slightly beaten

1 can corn kernel, drained

300 grams red bell pepper

200 grams green peas

300 grams green beans cut 1 inch long

Patis and black pepper to taste

2 tablespoons spring onion, chopped

Garnish:

wansoy, chopped

cucumber, cubed

tomato, seeded and cubed

1. Pre-heat saucepan, melt butter and stir-fry garlic until golden brown.

2. Remove garlic from pan and set aside.

3. Sauté onion and tanglad. Add sugar, tomato sauce, oyster sauce, and crab meat. Mix well.

4. Add bell pepper, green peas, green beans, and corn.

5. Flake rice before adding in the pan. Mix well.

6. Add eggs and continue mixing.

7. Season with patis and pepper.

8. Garnish with spring onion, wansoy, cucumber, tomatoes and fried garlic. Serve hot.

Tip: This is a meal in itself. Pair it with simple fried fish like daing or tinapa.

NILASING NA LAMBAY

(*DRUNKEN CRABS*)

4 crabs, cut in half

1 thumb-sized ginger, crushed

2 stalks lemongrass, bulb part crushed

1 cup coconut milk

1 cup coconut cream

½ cup bahalina (native wine from coconut)

3-5 sili labuyo (chilli peppers)

1 tablespoon achuete oil

1 bundle string beans, cut into 2" length

2 red bell peppers, sliced

2 tablespoons spring onion, chopped

Salt

1. In a saucepan, combine crabs, ginger, lemongrass and coconut milk.

2. Bring to a boil and lower heat. Simmer 5 minutes.

3. Add bahalina, siling labuyo, salt, achuete, string beans and simmer for 5 minutes.

4. Stir in coconut cream, bell pepper and spring onion. Simmer for another 5 minutes. Serve hot.

Tip: Lasing in Filipino is "drunk".

PATIO ILIJAN CRAB PACKETS

4 pieces young banana leaf, heated over fire to soften

4 crabs, remove top shell and legs

4 native pechay (Chinese cabbage), separate leaves

4 teaspoons ginger, grated

4 teaspoons spring onion, chopped

1 cup coconut cream

1 cup coconut milk

Salt to taste

1.   On a banana leaf, place 3 pechay leaves.

2.   Put 1 crab including crab fat on top of pechay.

3.   Season with salt, 1 teaspoon grated ginger, and 1 teaspoon spring onion.

4.   Carefully pour 2 tablespoons coconut cream and wrap envelope-style.

5.   Tie with banana leaf segment.

6. Wrap remaining 3 crabs the same way.

7. Arrange wrapped crabs in a carajay and pour 1 cup of coconut milk.

8. Cover tightly and let boil. Lower heat and simmer for 30 minutes.

Tip: Do not discard the top shell and legs as it can still be used to make crab broth.

SPICY CRABS IN BLACK BEAN SAUCE

4 crabs, cut in half

½ cup soy sauce

1 head garlic, minced

1 onion, chopped

2 tablespoons ginger strips

1 tablespoon brown sugar

½ cup black beans mashed in 2 tablespoons vinegar

3-5 sili labuyo (chilli peppers), chopped

2 tablespoons cooking oil

¼ kilo okra, steamed

1. Heat oil in a wok, and sauté garlic, ginger and onion until wilted.

2. Add black beans in vinegar.

3. Add crabs and simmer for 2 minutes.

4. Add soy sauce, sugar and sili.

5. Mix well and simmer until done.

6. Serve hot with steamed okra on the side.

Tip: You can also add cubes of tofu.

STEAMED CRABS WITH PICKLED UBOD

PICKLED UBOD:

1 kilo ubod (heart of palm)

1 carrot, cut into strips

1 tablespoon ginger, strips

1 onion, sliced

1 head of garlic, sliced

3 pieces sili labuyo (chilli peppers)

1 cup sugar

2 teaspoons salt

1 cup vinegar

1. In a saucepan, heat sugar, salt, and vinegar and bring to a boil.

2. Pour over the other ingredients.

3. Set aside.

STEAMED CRABS:

4 crabs

1 cup 7 Up or Sprite

1 teaspoon salt

1. Put crabs upside-down in a saucepan.

2. Sprinkle salt and add 7 Up.

3. Cover and cook over low fire for 15 to 20 minutes.

4. Serve hot with pickled ubod on the side.

Tip: You can also steam mussels this way. Sometimes, we add for a more flavorful broth.

STUFFED CRAB SHELL

10 crabs, medium to large

1 onion, grated

½ cup carrot, grated

1 bell pepper, finely chopped

10 native chicken eggs or quail eggs

5 calamansi (Philippine lime), sliced

Margarine

Italian seasoning

Salt

Pepper

1. Steam crabs. Reserve shell, remove flesh and set aside.

2. In a bowl, mix crabmeat, onion, carrot, bell pepper, lemongrass, salt and pepper.

3. Separate egg yolks from white. Beat egg whites until stiff.

4. Add egg whites to crab mixture to bind.

5. Fill the shells with mixture, but take care not to overstuff.

6. At the center of each shell, press thumb to make a hole big enough for the yolk to fit.

7. Brush the top filling with margarine. Sprinkle with Italian seasoning.

8. Fill each hole with yolk.

9. Steam 10 to 15 minutes over low fire.

10. Serve on bed of lettuce.

11. Sprinkle with calamansi juice before serving.

Tip: This will look pretty over a simple noodle or pasta dish.

Maxima Magsalin-Ricafort retired to Ilijan Norte, Tubigon, Bohol to live a stress-free and pollution-free life with her husband after their three daughters finished college. They are currently helping the dairy farmers in the community establish fresh milk processing as a sustainable livelihood in Tubigon. She has also served Serviam Catholic Charismatic Community and Bukas Loob sa Diyos Community since 1990.

Maxima is now working on Volume 2 of her Crab Recipes.